Original title:
Shadows Beneath the Sycamores

Copyright © 2025 Creative Arts Management OÜ
All rights reserved.

Author: Ophelia Ravenscroft
ISBN HARDBACK: 978-1-80567-401-6
ISBN PAPERBACK: 978-1-80567-700-0

Glimmers of Hope Among the Roots

In the park where the squirrels play,
A raccoon danced, stealing the day.
With acorns piled high as a mound,
He snagged a snack, lost his ground.

Laughter rang out in the breeze,
As birds chirped tunes, doing as they please.
The sun peeked through leaves with a grin,
While ants marched like they were set to win.

A dog rolled over in ripe delight,
Chasing his tail with all of his might.
Hilarious slips on the grassy plain,
Every tumble gave giggles a gain.

In nature's circus, the fun won't cease,
Every creature a jester, bringing us peace.
With glimmers of hope in each burst of cheer,
We'll dance under laughter as long as we're here.

Tales Woven in Natural Light

Beneath the shade, where wild things roam,
A clever raccoon called it home.
He donned a hat made from leaves and twine,
Trading acorns for stories, feeling just fine.

The rabbit wore glasses, quite the scholar,
Lecturing wise, with a hop and a holler.
While turtles slowly pondered each phrase,
In the natural light, they basked in the haze.

The wind played tricks, tangled the hair,
Of a fox who thought she was quite the fair.
With a twirl and a whirl, she danced 'round the tree,
Chasing her dreams with mischievous glee.

As laughter erupted from critters so bright,
Their tales intertwined, woven in light.
Each creature a character, strange but so right,
Under the canopy, the world felt just right.

Tracing the Lines of Light

In a park where squirrels prance,
A cat in shades does a little dance.
Beneath the leaves where giggles bloom,
Lies a secret place that spells out 'room.'

With a hop and skip, a frog jumps high,
Winking at a bird that forgot how to fly.
Sunbeams twist, they tickle and tease,
While ants in line march with great ease.

Ethereal Breaths of a Leafy Sanctuary

A breeze whispers jokes only trees can hear,
As acorns fall, causing much raucous cheer.
Chipmunks gossip in a chittering spree,
While branches wave cheerfully, laughing with glee.

The wind plays tag with a wobbly twig,
As bees buzz along, doing a happy jig.
An owl in the distance hoots just for fun,
His riddle-filled wisdom leaves everyone stunned.

The Melody of Rustling Underfoot

Crunchy leaves compose a silly tune,
As footsteps dance beneath the crescent moon.
A raccoon runs by, wearing a hat too small,
He tips it politely, then stumbles and sprawls.

Under the boughs, a family picnics,
Spilling their juice and making some gimmicks.
Laughter erupts like a geyser in spring,
Even the trees can't help but swing.

The Pulse of the Eternal Grove

In the heart of the woods, where laughter ignites,
A plush bear conducts tree concerts at nights.
A tumbleweed rolls by, chasing a whim,
While crickets play tunes on a breeze quite dim.

Old trunks share tales of the past with a wave,
Of treasure hunts lost and the friendships they save.
In this quirky realm where nature takes flight,
Every moment's a jest—a whimsical sight.

Remnants of Daylight's Glow

As the sun bids its cheeky goodbye,
A squirrel sneaks by, oh my, oh my!
Chasing its tail in a wild, goofy race,
It trips on a root, what a clumsy embrace!

The light flickers low, but giggles remain,
A rabbit in sunglasses, feeling no pain.
With friends in tow, they hop and they play,
Dancing on grass, come join the ballet!

Hidden Stories in the Bark

If trees could giggle, oh the tales they'd spin,
Of acorns that fell, and the squirrels' win.
One nutty old oak scribbles with glee,
'Last week, a raccoon tried dressing like me!'

In soft whispers, the branches conspire,
Raccoons and rabbits, all aiming higher.
The owls roll their eyes at the antics so bold,
'These kids have no sense; they do what they're told!'

Shades of Time in the Forest's Heart

Time wobbles funny, like a bouncy ball,
Trees counting giggles, they watch, stand tall.
The breeze plays tag with leaves in delight,
While the sun juggles stars; it's a curious sight!

Old roots tell secrets of mischief and fun,
Of frogs in bow ties, ready to run.
They leap like madmen, in froggy ballet,
A stage made of moss, who needs Broadway?

Unraveled Threads of Evening

Evening unravels, with laughter galore,
A hedgehog with shades, can't take it anymore!
He rolls down the hill, his spines all a-flop,
While fireflies giggle, they'll never stop!

With every tickle of twilight so sweet,
The critters come out; it's a jolly retreat.
From dancing in circles, to silly old games,
They blend into dusk, and their joy never wanes!

Tales Inscribed in the Bark

Once a squirrel had a plan,
To carve his name with pride.
But the bark was rough and tough,
He slipped, fell, and just... sighed.

His friends rolled on the ground,
Laughter echoing near,
While he mumbled through his frown,
"Next time, I'll stick to cheer!"

A raccoon with a paintbrush,
Dotted leaves in green and gold.
Made a masterpiece—just once,
So the story has been told.

Now we gather where he slipped,
And gaze at that old tree.
Wondering where those acorns went,
And if he'll climb just to see!

Resilience of the Ancient Guardians

Beneath the giant branches sway,
A family of ants does prance.
Each leaf a disco, wild and free,
While nature gives them the chance.

They march in sync, a funny sight,
With tiny hats made from grass.
A dance party in full delight,
While time, it seems, will not pass.

"Watch out for that puddle!" they yell,
But it's too late for their shoes.
They wade through like it's a swell,
Giggling as they choose to lose!

So under leafy, boughs they sway,
The guardians laugh at the fuss.
For life is wild and full of play,
And that's just how it must be for us!

The Allure of Dappled Paths

Under sunlight's playful wink,
A rabbit hops with flair.
Twisting, turning without a blink,
As if performing in midair.

A turtle looks upon the show,
With utmost calm and grace.
"Fast isn't always the way to go,
I'll win this silly race."

The rabbit stops, all out of breath,
"Oh wait! You've passed me by!"
While squirrels chase the winds of death,
And giggling catch their sighs.

So paths are filled with funny friends,
In dappled light, they play.
They dance and bounce till daylight ends,
And let laughter rule the day!

Past Lives in the Timber's Shade

Once a raccoon with a dream,
Thought he could fly like a bird.
In a hat made from leaves, on a beam,
He swooped down, but not as he heard.

A bat looked on with a laugh,
"Too much ambition, my friend!"
While the raccoon flailed, fell on his staff,
"Let's call this a trend!"

From roots to branches, a tale well spun,
Of what might have been, oh so grand.
Life's twists and turns—just for fun,
As we take it all as planned.

These ancient giants hold us close,
With memories wrapped like a quilt.
They whisper jokes—life's uproarious prose,
In every heart, laughter is built!

Flickering Silhouettes of Time

In a park where squirrels prance,
A dog thinks it's a dance.
Trees with knotty knees do sway,
As leaves gossip and play.

Beneath the branches, shadows creep,
Lurching like they've missed their leap.
Tickling grass that's trying to sleep,
In a game, we'll never keep.

A child jumps high to touch the blue,
While a bee claims the flowers too.
Laughter bursts through a tiny crack,
As ants march in a gentle pack.

Leaves fall like a mad confetti,
As everyone starts to get petty.
In the whimsy of this place,
We lose ourselves in nature's grace.

The Enigmas of Rustic Light

A mouse wearing a tiny hat,
Questions all the things we spat.
Amidst the light that comes and goes,
Chasing every curious nose.

Cows gather round, eyes ever wide,
Wondering who's their farmer's pride.
The barn stands tall, full of tales,
As chicken flaps its feathered sails.

Sunbeams wiggle through the trees,
Causing sleepy bugs to sneeze.
The old dog snores without a care,
As laughter mingles in the air.

Footsteps echo, lost in mirth,
As shadows spin back to their birth.
In this laughter-drenched delight,
The world seems oddly just right.

Cradled in Nature's Embrace

A cat ponders between two fences,
Plotting pounce while upending senses.
Flowers giggle at butterflies' dance,
In this garden, luck finds a chance.

The pond is a mirror, oh so sly,
Reflecting thoughts of fish that fly.
Tadpoles wear goggles, swim with glee,
While frogs in toads are two-fold free.

Worms argue over who eats best,
While the sun takes its cozy rest.
A haphazard picnic makes its mark,
Where ants line up, a fine spark.

In a world of green and gold,
Every moment's a tale untold.
As laughter rolls like an old stone,
In nature's arms, we're not alone.

Twilight Dances on Forgotten Trails

As dusk unfolds its velvet cape,
A ladybug dons her own escape.
Crickets serenade the moon's light,
While fireflies dress in bold midnight.

Old boots on paths of tangled dreams,
Trip over roots, the forest beams.
Each twist of trail tells tales anew,
Step by step, we're drawn into view.

Hooting owls play peek-a-boo,
While raccoons debate what's true.
The stars twinkle with mischief untold,
In this twilight where stories unfold.

Under the blanket of twilight's charm,
We skip along with no alarm.
In forgotten places, laughter ignites,
As shadows turn into playful sights.

Echoes of a Hidden Life

In the park where squirrels prance,
A raccoon dons a brazen stance,
They grab sandwiches from a pack,
While giggles echo through the crack.

A couple dancing near the stream,
Tripped on roots, oh what a dream!
They flail like fish out of the sea,
The crickets chirp in pure glee.

Beneath the trees, a cactus hat,
Worn by a forgetful cat,
It struts along, so full of pride,
While laughter rolls like a joyful tide.

At dusk, the shadows twist and twirl,
Where mischief found a playful whirl,
Glimpses of bees in tiny bows,
They dance their way where no one knows.

Ephemeral Wonders in a Sunlit Glade

A frog with headphones on so tight,
Disco dances in the light,
While butterflies in sequined wings,
Are laughing hard at silly things.

The sunbeams peek through leaves so wide,
As children giggle, run, and slide,
An ice cream cone, it tips and falls,
Creating joy in summer calls.

A bear in overalls so bright,
Tries to assemble a kite in flight,
It soars high, then comes down fast,
He hides his face, but not his laugh!

The ladybugs declare a race,
While ants join in with tiny grace,
They zoom past grass blades, what a sight,
Under canopies, a funny night.

Murmurs of the Verdant Veil

Within the leaves, a secret lies,
A parakeet with comic eyes,
He tells the tales of silly lore,
In whispers soft, their spirits soar.

A hedgehog with a tiny cap,
Struts along in rhythmic clap,
While turtles laugh at snail's slow pace,
They all join in the merry race.

The sunlight flickers, teasingly,
As frogs conduct a philharmony,
The wind joins in, a gentle breeze,
A symphony among the trees.

In hidden spots, where laughter grows,
The forest blooms with chuckling prose,
Each rustle, giggle, scurrying feet,
Leaves behind a joy so sweet.

The Lilt of Lost Footsteps

A path where shout and whimsy meet,
Two raccoons mumble by the street,
They dance in pairs, like waltzing pros,
As skunks roll over, strike a pose.

The daisies nod, with heads so bright,
While bees are buzzing pure delight,
An old dog snores, he's had his fill,
Of chasing, playing, oh what a thrill!

A chipmunk dons a tiny hat,
While spider silk holds up the chat,
They gossip, giggle, and share their dreams,
Under the glint of sunlight beams.

The night unfolds with hidden jest,
A chorus sings, they don their best,
With laughter twirling round each bend,
This woodland fun will never end.

Celestial Glimmers in Leafy Halls

In the park where squirrels prance,
Dancing leaves play a merry dance,
Acorns drop, and giggles swell,
Nature's secrets, oh so swell.

Sunbeams peek through branches wide,
As birds chirp songs of joy and pride,
A bear plays hide and seek with bees,
While rabbits munch on dandelion leaves.

Pine cones plop like clumsy balls,
Making children laugh in fits and sprawls,
Twirling leaves in a breezy whirl,
Every twist brings a new pearl.

Among the trees, mischief reigns,
As bugs throw parties, ignoring stains,
The laughter echoes, pure and bright,
In leafy halls of sheer delight.

The Legacy of Ancient Pathways

Old trails weave through trees so tall,
Whispers of secrets, a nature hall,
Raccoons debating snack choices right,
While owls judge from a grassy height.

Each step reveals a comical mime,
As bushes gossip about the time,
When woodpeckers played a game of tag,
And frogs sent each other off with a brag.

The past holds tales of silly plays,
Like turtles stuck in romantic daze,
Chasing butterflies, oh what a sight,
In the great outdoors, everything's bright.

Along these trails we stroll so free,
With laughter shared between you and me,
Footprints of joy left in the dust,
Echoing fun, in nature we trust.

Shadows of Memory in the Underbrush

Beneath the leaves where critters dwell,
There lurks a tale that time will tell,
Of forgotten snacks and playful pranks,
By those who frolic beside sunlit banks.

A chipmunk frets o'er a lost pine nut,
While hedgehogs put on a silly strut,
Over rocks and logs, in vain they race,
Chasing the breeze, each laugh a trace.

The underbrush, a stage for glee,
Where stories twist like a wild tree,
Bunnies hop high with giggly grace,
Creating joy in this green space.

In this cozy nook, all's absurd,
Nature's comic play, unseen, unheard,
Histories blend with the rustling leaves,
A jester's realm where mirth believes.

Harmony in Solitude's Cradle

In solitude, the breeze has fun,
With whispers tickling everyone,
Dancing grass sways with flair and ease,
While whispers merge with buzzing bees.

A lonely rock hosts a lizard's line,
Who sunbathes boldly, thinking divine,
A sleepy cat naps on sunlit moss,
While fireflies swirl, ignoring the cost.

Leaves hold secrets from ages past,
Of quirky creatures, first and last,
Each rustle a chuckle, of playful delight,
A gathering of friends in the soft twilight.

Here in quiet, the laughter grows,
As nature giggles and softly glows,
In this cradle of calm and cheer,
Mirth springs up, so loud and clear.

Enchanted Corners of the Wild

In the wild where the critters dance,
A squirrel in a hat takes a chance.
He wears his acorn like a crown,
While birds in bow ties gather 'round.

A rabbit with glasses reads a book,
The stories he tells got everyone shook.
A raccoon with a lute begins to strum,
And soon the whole forest is having fun.

In corners where secrets softly bide,
A gnome in a hammock takes a slide.
With laughter echoing through the trees,
Even the ants are laughing with ease.

The fawns play chess, the fox won't stop,
With paws in the air, he's ready to hop.
The woodland ball's a sight to behold,
With creatures in costumes, brave and bold.

Soft Heartbeats of the Understory

Down low where the petals flirt,
A snail's got speed in a fancy shirt.
He zooms past a worm in a race,
Who's got the slowest, silliest face.

A hedgehog in boots gives a grin,
While bees buzz around him, dancing in spin.
They're thankful for honey, a sweet, sticky treat,
And they joke that it's better than anything to eat.

A frog in a bowler sings a tune,
Making frogs laugh 'til it's well past noon.
A party beneath where the shadows play,
Where humor and nature blend in a fray.

The butterflies flutter, the grasshoppers cheer,
With ticklish tickles making giggles appear.
A gathering so bright, what a way to thrive,
In soft heartbeats where laughter comes alive.

Echoes Weaved in Nature's Fabric

In threads of green, the stories twine,
A weasel finds cheese and thinks it divine.
He tells his pals, it's a stinky delight,
With a wink at the owl, who grins with delight.

The beavers are crafting a dam quite absurd,
While a squirrel steals snacks, not one bit deterred.
With giggles and chatter, they boast their great plans,
And laugh at their antics till the sun sets and spans.

A butterfly swoops in with a splendid wig,
Leaves the ladybugs saying, "That's quite big!"
They seek inspiration, a fashion parade,
In echoes of nature where silliness played.

A turtle on roller skates, what a sight!
He waves to a rabbit who's flying a kite.
In laughter and fun, the forest's a stage,
In nature's grand fabric, we all engage.

Fables of the Wisest Canopy

In the canopy high, there's wisdom, they say,
With owls giving lectures at the end of the day.
A squirrel in glasses leads a wild class,
While the trees whisper secrets, their wisdom amassed.

A raccoon in a robe plays the part of a sage,
With tales of the acorn that won him a wage.
Telling fables of bravery, absurdity too,
The critters come flocking, excited for new.

With branches a-twisting, winds blow through fast,
They join in the laughter, let good times last.
While the hedgehogs debate the best way to eat,
A porcupine shouts, "Let's dance on our feet!"

Amidst all the giggles of wisdom profound,
The canopy sways, a party unbound.
For in nature's tales, with humor so bright,
The wisest of critters take flight in the night.

Whispers of Twilight Leaves

In the quiet drops of dusk,
The squirrels start to fuss,
With acorns flying left and right,
As critters prepare for dinner's bite.

Leaves giggle in the breeze,
Tickling branches, oh what tease!
A rabbit trips, lands in a pile,
Chasing shadows, all the while.

The owl hoots, a cheeky sound,
While the baby deer twirls around,
Mischief stirs in nature's glow,
As twilight whispers soft and low.

Fireflies twinkle, bright and bold,
Dancing tales of jokes untold,
As laughter echoes, softly flows,
In the realm where fun just grows.

Echoes in the Canopy

Beneath the boughs, where lovers meet,
A raccoon stumbles on its feet,
With a waddle and a clumsy spin,
It steals a snack and thinks it wins.

The woodpecker, quite the chap,
Knocks on trees, a comic rap,
While chipmunks mimic in delight,
Causing giggles in the night.

A breeze that whispers, tickles too,
The branches sway, they dance and skew,
A game of tag, a playful race,
In this hardwood circus space.

Echoes bounce, create a tune,
As critters laugh by the light of the moon,
So come and join this jolly scene,
Where nature laughs, and we're all keen.

Secrets of the Ancient Grove

Locked within the gnarled trees,
Lies a tale that stirs the breeze,
The mischievous fox plays the spy,
With a wink and a quirk of its eye.

Old turtles share their sage advice,
About the joys of rolling dice,
As dragonflies tease from above,
Painting the air with sprightly love.

The hedgehog wears a tiny crown,
Patrolling eaves with a quirky frown,
While wisps of laughter float and twirl,
In the forest, where pranks unfurl.

The trees conspire, giggling low,
Nature's jesters, putting on a show,
With whispers shared and smiles anew,
In this grove of secrets, welcome to you.

Dappled Dreams on Soft Earth

In the dappling light, dreams take flight,
As bunnies hop in sheer delight,
They spring and bounce, a funny scene,
Wearing tiny hats, oh how they preen!

The raccoons, with swagger and style,
Plan a heist with a cheeky smile,
Stealing pies from a picnic spread,
While the owls just shake their heads.

A silky web, a spider's pride,
Catches unexpected flies inside,
As bees buzz low, sharing jokes,
Creating laughter 'tween the oaks.

In this whimsical world of mirth,
Where nature celebrates its birth,
Laughter dances like the sun,
In dreams embraced, we all are one.

Quiet Grace in the Dusk

In twilight's soft embrace, we sway,
A squirrel steals a snack, then runs away.
The fireflies dance with all their might,
While crickets serenade into the night.

With branches bent from too much weight,
How did that one tree get such a fate?
A raccoon peeks with a glint of pride,
Seeking a dinner he knows he'll find.

Laughter lingers in the cool air,
As friends recount stories, each one a flair.
The world feels lighter under this hush,
Like nature's gossip in a friendly rush.

So gather 'round, the dusk is our stage,
Where even tall tales come of age.
Under limbs that lean, so sweetly bend,
In the fading light, where giggles blend.

Beneath the Breaths of Old Trees

A whirlwind of leaves in a playful chase,
Old trees shake hands in a leafy embrace.
With roots that tickle the earth's hidden grin,
They whisper secrets of where they've been.

A daring bird shows off a plucky flair,
While a busy ant marches without a care.
Each rustling leaf has stories untold,
Of pranks and mischief from ages of old.

The moon peeks through like a curious friend,
Illuminating paths where laughter won't end.
In the chorus of night, we find our place,
As creatures of whimsy join the race.

Nature chuckles, a gentle tease,
Sprinkling balmy nights with a hint of ease.
So let us indulge in this frolicsome spree,
Beneath the breaths of what else could be.

Tales Carved in Nature's Memory

The gnarled branches tell of lost escapades,
Of playful children in sunlight parades.
Each knot and twist holds a laugh or two,
In the silent woods where mischief grew.

A fox passes by with stealthy grace,
While the raccoons sneak snacks from their place.
Beneath the canopy of whispers and cheer,
The earth chuckles softly for all who draw near.

In this wild theater where nature takes flight,
Even shadows join in, adding to the delight.
With rustles and giggles, the night merges on,
In a world of wonder until the dawn.

So tune in your heart to the music of trees,
Their laughter will dance in the cool evening breeze.
With stories carved deep, they invite you to see,
The charm and the joy of wild memory.

Glimmers of Hope in the Gloom

When nightfall creeps in with a playful shove,
Stars giggle softly, as if in love.
They wink and they blink, a mischievous sight,
Guiding our dreams through the quiet night.

The owls hoot jokes from the branches above,
As creatures below share a story of love.
With shadows that flicker and dance on the ground,
Even the silly can always be found.

Between laughter and sighs, the night flows on,
With echoes of folly till the break of dawn.
In this cozy gloom, adventure ignites,
As whispers of hope take flight in the nights.

So gather your friends, let the fun abound,
In moonlit whispers, where joy is unbound.
With each little chuckle, we weave a grand tune,
In glimmers of hope beneath watchful moon.

Ghostly Traces of the Day

In the woods where owls hoot
A squirrel steals a pirate's loot
Fallen acorns roll and bounce
While rabbits hold a secret pounce.

The sun dips low, the giggles fly
As fireflies dance and tease the sky
A ghostly waltz of leaves that spin
While owls plot how to sneak their win.

Raccoons wear masks like bandits bold
Stealing snacks and tales retold
But in this merry woodland game
No one is ever quite the same.

So here's to laughter in retreat
Where nature's pranks are quite the feat
Amidst the trees, a joyful cheer
For ghostly traces linger near!

The Solitude of Silent Leaves

A leaf fell down with quite a thud
And whispered stories in the mud
A laughter slipped from bough to ground
Where silly secrets swirled around.

With every breeze, a ticklish kiss
The critters plot a leafy bliss
A silent leaf, it starts to dance
In nature's grand comedic chance.

The crunch of twigs, a startled sound
As woodland creatures jostle 'round
They giggle at their silly fate
And turn the quiet into late.

So come, dear friend, let's join the fun
In solitude where laughter's spun
Among the leaves that dance and sway
Their silent giggles light the day!

Beneath the Arching Boughs

Under branches stretching wide
A band of mischief starts to hide
With acorns tucked in every nook
They swap their tales like storybooks.

A rabbit hops with quite a flair
Cackling madly, without a care
He juggles nuts like circus seals
While watching out for sneaky heels.

The wise old owl just shakes his head
As squirrels plot from branch to bed
A grand parade of silly tales
While twirling down on leafy trails.

So let's rejoice beneath the trees
With playful tricks and giggles, please
For every twist, a laugh anew
In nature's comedy, we're the crew!

Enigmas in the Woodland's Heart

In the heart where whispers twine
A raccoon leans, a cup of wine
He raises brows, with sleight of paw
As if to decipher this strange law.

The woods confess their little quirks
With every rustle, laughter jerks
A hedgehog snorts, a turtle grins
While woodland creatures share their sins.

A fox appears with poker face
As if he's won a funny race
His tail held high, all fluff and pride
In riddles where the giggles hide.

So join the fun with gleeful heart
In woodland journeys, laughter's art
With enigmas painting every hue
In nature's jest, our spirits flew!

Fluttering Spirits Among the Fronds

In a grove where giggles play,
Leaves dance in a breezy sway.
Squirrels wear their acorn hats,
Chasing dreams of chubby rats.

Butterflies in polka dots,
Play hide and seek with tiny tots.
Laughter bubbles, filled with cheer,
While crickets sing to passing deer.

A raccoon juggles fallen pine,
While birds all chirp, 'You're so divine!'
The sun peeks through just to tease,
As nature giggles in the breeze.

So come and dance beneath the green,
Where life's a laugh, a joyful scene.
Each rustling leaf a secret told,
In playful whispers, brave and bold.

The Hushed Watcher Beneath the Canopy

A grumpy owl upon a branch,
Hoots at squirrels with a chance.
He rolls his eyes, so very wise,
At rabbits with their fuss and lies.

Beneath the boughs, the shadows leap,
As ants parade, their treasures heap.
The chatter of the breeze is sweet,
While crickets tap their tiny feet.

A turtle yawns, all slow and grand,
While frogs discuss their lily-land.
The world below a giggling show,
As breezes play with nature's flow.

And if you listen, you might hear,
A giggle or a whispered cheer.
For life's a joke, a vibrant jest,
Under the trees, we live our best.

Nature's Nostalgic Embrace

The wind hums tunes of days gone by,
As daisies wink beneath the sky.
Old acorns laugh at their own fate,
While sunbeams weave through leaves and mate.

A rabbit recalls his younger days,
When he could hop in joyful ways.
Now he twitches, quite austere,
As youth fades like a fleeting year.

The brook babbles secrets too,
While minnows show off in their view.
Twirls and jumps in merry glee,
Nature's dance is wild and free.

Oh, how they cherish all that's lost,
But laughter shines despite the cost.
In every pause, a memory glows,
In nature's arms, where laughter flows.

Ripples of the Forgotten Grove

In an old grove where whispers dwell,
Laughter echoes, can you tell?
Frogs play leapfrog on the logs,
While turtles roll like tiny dogs.

The wind carries tales of old,
Of flowers bright and laughter bold.
An opossum grins, quite a sight,
Counting stars in the cool night light.

With every rustle, stories thrive,
In nature's dream, they feel alive.
A merry band of critters play,
In that special, secret way.

So if you wander, take a peek,
Where giggles hide and nature speaks.
The grove's alive, a vibrant spree,
In ripples of lost memory.

The Stillness Between Suns

In the gap where jesters hide,
A picnic basket near, they bide.
Juggling fruits with endless glee,
Laughing loud beneath the tree.

With squirrels sneaking bits of cake,
Each crumb is met with a cheeky shake.
A game of tag with shadows played,
As the sun and giggles cascade.

A soft breeze whispers silly tunes,
While bees attempt to dance with spoons.
Oh, the mischief hidden there,
In stillness, laughter fills the air!

So toast the day with silly cheer,
Laugh until the sky is clear.
In the calm, let joy ignite,
Between the suns, it all feels right!

Mysterious Paths of Tranquil Light

A winding trail of whimsy calls,
With babbling brooks and playful falls.
The sunbeams curl, they tease and twine,
As frogs wear hats and sip on brine.

A rabbit hops with flair so grand,
Wearing mismatched socks, how dandy!
The path is paved with giggles bright,
Where every turn brings pure delight.

Chasing fireflies that dance and wink,
With every hop, they pause to think.
Is it magic, or just good fun?
Paths of light till day is done!

So join the dance, the joyous jest,
In this wild, enchanted quest.
With laughter bright and spirits light,
In tranquil light, all is just right!

Veils of Memory in the Glade

In a glade draped with stories old,
Where leaves murmur secrets untold.
A ticklish breeze from ancient years,
Brings forth laughter, yields to cheers.

The statues grin with playful eyes,
As ants march by in silly ties.
Fog here dances, twirls with grace,
While a raccoon dreams of the race.

With giggles echoing through the mist,
And whispers of a prank at dusk,
Time bends, and here's the catch,
Memories blend with the fun we hatch.

So gather round, let stories weave,
In this glade, we won't believe.
With heart and humor always laid,
In veils of joy, our dreams are made!

Beneath the Whispering Boughs

Under branches where secrets sigh,
The squirrels plot with a knowing eye.
They share the tales of nutty finds,
As laughter ripples through their minds.

A cat with shades lounges with flair,
While birds narrate the latest dare.
A game of hide and seek does start,
Beneath the boughs, where giggles dart.

With shadows prancing, dancing round,
The twist of fate is joy unbound.
Each giggle hides a lingering jest,
Beneath the canopy, we feel blessed.

So join the whimsy in this space,
Where fun and friendship interlace.
With each soft whisper and playful sound,
In laughter's hearth, our hearts are found!

Lullabies of the Oak and Elm

Beneath branches swaying, a squirrel does sing,
Chasing its tail in spring's funny fling.
A hole in a trunk, a raccoon peeks out,
Wondering if dinner's a picnic or shout.

In the shade of the leaves, the owls do jest,
Telling tall tales of the eagle's best quest.
A chipmunk with acorns, so proud of his load,
Trips on a route that each critter has trod.

With laughter that echoes from roots down below,
The tickling breeze plays a whimsical show.
As the sun makes its rounds, the forest's alive,
In a dance of the trees, all creatures arrive.

A snail tells a story that only slows down,
While grasshoppers leap in a comedic crown.
In this leafy realm, where the giggles don't cease,
Every flap and each scurry is a song of peace.

The Lurking Mysteries of Green

In the depths of the woods, there's mystery near,
Where the frogs throw their hats like a costumed cheer.
A squirrel with sunglasses pretends to be cool,
While the turtles just laugh, 'They can't even drool!'

Beneath the green cover, a wild boar rolls by,
Covered in mud with a glint in his eye.
He snorts at the owl who just juggles a worm,
And the laughter erupts, oh, the tales that they churn!

The insects all gossip about things they have seen,
Like that time someone splashed in the river so mean.
A dance-off ensues on the forest's damp floor,
Where the beetles show moves like you've never seen before!

And as twilight drapes its soft twilight cloak,
The crickets recite lines that make the trees choke.
In this strange, silly land where the humor is keen,
Every shimmy and shake is a wink in the green.

Flickering Hues of Past Lives

In colors that twinkle, the memories play,
Of flowers once blooming, all gone but the sway.
A butterfly chuckles, as it flits with great glee,
"Can you believe that? A cactus talked to me!"

The old logs whisper with stories from yore,
Of raccoons that pranced and danced on the floor.
The moss wears a grin like it's hiding a scheme,
While sunlight bursts forth in a light-hearted dream.

The shadows collect, like cousins in chairs,
Telling tall tales about old forest fairs.
A bear in a tutu, oh what a bizarre sight,
Crafting a ballet under the moonlight bright!

Here in this realm, where the laughter is free,
Every rustle and giggle sets the critters' hearts free.
While echoes of past flicker with whimsy and cheer,
The forest retails tales we hold ever dear.

Beneath the Arch of Leafy Dream

Under an arch where the sunbeams peek,
The rabbits hold parties, oh what a cheek!
With hats made of clovers and tails all a-fluff,
They dance on the grass, saying, "This is enough!"

A weasel in stripes tells the best of his jokes,
While the raccoons cackle, oh how it provokes!
The butterflies flutter in laughter and pose,
Who knew such fun thrived beneath leafy prose?

Now watch as the hedgehog dons a top hat,
Strutting his stuff to a rat-tat-tat!
The critters all cheer, as they throw seeds in the air,
Creating a wonderland without a single care.

So come join the ruckus where giggles abound,
In this realm of delight, magic knows no bound.
For beneath the green arch, where the fun does gleam,
Lies the heart of the forest, a whimsical dream.

The Fabric of Dusk's Caress

In twilight's grip, squirrels dance,
Chasing dreams in a leafy trance.
A couple of owls, wise and sly,
Plotting mischief as fireflies fly.

A raccoon dips, stealing a snack,
While crickets perform, no need to pack.
Laughter spills as the stars peek through,
Nature's jest unfolds, a grand debut.

The breeze begins its playful tease,
Whispers secrets to rustling leaves.
A waltz of laughter, sweetened loam,
Beneath the tree, we've found our home.

As fireflies blink in a game of tag,
The night wears smiles, no moments drag.
In joyous glee, the critters prance,
Under the twilight, they take their chance.

Phantasms in the Twisted Trunk

Fanciful shapes in gnarled wood,
Critters creating a ruckus, pretty good.
The wind spins tales of the things they've seen,
In a bard's voice, they're the theater's queen.

The funky raccoon puts on a show,
Dancing like nobody's watching, you know.
The branches sway to an unseen beat,
And under the boughs, we shuffle our feet.

Then comes a fox with a mischievous grin,
Whispering secrets of places he's been.
With every laugh, the crickets join in,
A symphony born as the fun begins.

In shadows that play on the forest floor,
We find the magic we've been searching for.
A carnival blooms in the wood's embrace,
Where whimsy and laughter twirl in the space.

Vestiges of Time's Embrace

Leaves flutter down like confetti so bright,
Time's playful hand in the fading light.
A chipmunk scurries with nuts held tight,
In this comedy, every critter takes flight.

The trees hold gossip from ages gone by,
Mice take the stage, oh my, oh my!
While owls roll their eyes at the silly fray,
As twilight giggles, it steals hearts away.

Laughter echoes as shadows take bow,
In this grand orchestration of the now.
Nature's jesters, with twirls and spins,
Celebrate life where the fun begins.

With a brushstroke of night, the antics grow,
Creating scenes only the wild could know.
In this small theater of leaf and bark,
The humor of dusk ignites the dark.

Portraits of the Fading Light

As daylight wanes, the laughter flows,
With frolicsome friends in a thicket that glows.
A frog on a log croaks out a tune,
While fireflies twinkle, an endearing boon.

An owl in the tree tries on different looks,
With a monocle perched, he reads ancient books.
The critters gather, applauding the sight,
In the gallery wrought from the fading light.

Squirrels don hats made from acorn caps,
Planning adventures and cheeky mishaps.
As night unfolds with a chuckle and cheer,
The art of the dusk draws everyone near.

With every giggle, the faces glow bright,
In the canvas of dusk, what a splendid sight.
As we wander through tales spun from delight,
We lose track of time in the shimmering night.

Echoing Footsteps Where Light Fades

In the park after dark, they roam,
A band of squirrels, far from home.
Chasing shadows, to and fro,
Whispering secrets only they know.

The echoes bounce off every tree,
What could that be? A ghostly spree!
Laughter erupts as they chase the night,
A raccoon joins in; oh what a sight!

With goofy bounds, and leaps so bold,
The tales they share, are quite untold.
In the fading light, frolic and play,
No one will catch them; they're too far away.

Underneath the twinkling stars,
They sing of biscuits, and glorious cars.
A celebration of the twilight's grace,
In this whimsical, wacky, leafy place.

The Mystery of the Gnarled Roots

Once upon a time, in a garden so old,
Lived roots that twisted, a sight to behold.
They whispered loud, in a hushed, secretive tone,
"What mischief shall we claim as our own?"

A turtle approached, with a curious face,
He tiptoed around, his slow, steady pace.
"Do you think you can handle my crazy old friends?"
The roots giggled softly, this game never ends!

In a grand debate, they plotted and schemed,
For a wild party, or so it seemed.
"I'm bringing the snacks!" said the chubby old mole,
"Don't forget the music; let's rock and take roll!"

As night fell softly, the roots came alive,
With moonlight above, they danced, and they jived.
Though gnarled and twisted, they knew how to groove,
In a wacky world, they found their own move.

Twisted Memories in the Brush

In a brush so thick, where the critters play,
Funny memories tumble and sway.
A badger once brought a sandwich so grand,
But it vanished, oh what a comic misband!

A parade of ants, in a line so neat,
Stole crumbs from a picnic, a tasty sweet treat.
"Quick! Call the cheese!" the rabbit did shout,
While squirrels argued on who had the clout.

With stories that tangled like vines in a knot,
Each moment was wacky, each laugh quite a lot.
In the depths of the brush, under foliage wide,
They laughed till they cried, in the chaos they bide.

And so it goes on, in that marvelous place,
Where laughter and stories put smiles on each face.
Twisted memories, all filled with delight,
In the wild, whimsically echoing night.

A Symphony of Quietude

In the calm of the night, when the world sleeps tight,
A symphony brews in the absence of light.
Crickets play fiddles, the owl takes the stage,
While fireflies twinkle, the stars are their wage.

Amidst the stillness, a rustle is heard,
Two chipmunks bicker, it's quite absurd!
"Who took my acorn? It was my best stash!"
The other just laughs, "You ate it in a flash!"

As wind whispers softly through branches so wide,
The humor unfolds in this night's merry ride.
Each sound tells a joke, each rustle a spin,
In the quiet, they chuckle; let the fun begin!

So here in this glowing kaleidoscope light,
Sounds of nature form the chorus of night.
And if you listen closely, you might even hear,
The echoes of laughter, so joyous and near.

Soft Secrets of the Forest Floor

A squirrel scurries past my feet,
With acorns hoarded, quite the feat.
His cheeks puffed up, a sight so dear,
Who knew that nuts could bring such cheer?

The mushrooms giggle, wearing hats,
While ladybugs form quirky chats.
A rabbit bounces, jumps for joy,
With carrots hidden, oh what ploy!

In cozy nooks, the critters play,
Whispers of mischief fill the day.
Beneath the leaves, they skitter here,
And even crickets join in cheer!

Nature's secrets, light and free,
Twirling tales, oh can't you see?
In this playground, laughter reigns,
Where silly hearts break all the chains.

Nightfall's Gentle Tapestry

The fireflies blink like tiny stars,
They dance around, ignoring cars.
A raccoon dons a mask of pride,
As he rummages, he won't hide!

The owls hoot tunes of silly lore,
While frogs croak softly, begging for more.
A cat with sass, so full of grace,
Turns up its nose at this wild race!

The cool breeze whispers cheeky songs,
To fireflies twirling, they can't go wrong.
Amidst the trees, a party thrives,
With giggles echoing, nature jives!

As midnight falls, the charm does bloom,
A chorus rises from the gloom.
Stars wink down, with playful charm,
Enthralled by night's soft, silly calm.

The Dance of Time in Rustic Groves

The oak tree sways with whimsy tall,
While squirrels chatter, having a ball.
Old roots know tales of days gone by,
With leaves that rustle a giggly sigh!

The wind brings laughter, so sweet and clear,
As ants parade in a silly cheer.
Time skips along, a jolly friend,
In rustic groves, the fun won't end!

A butterfly flits in joyful flight,
Stirring giggles with pure delight.
In every crevice, life's quirkiness shows,
Even the stones have secrets that flow!

So join the dance of this merry place,
Where time is a jester with laughter's grace.
In every turn, through roots and leaves,
The joy of nature weaves what it believes.

Lost Tales of Nature's Keep

The brook giggles, splashing bright,
While turtles sunbathe, oh what a sight!
They've lost their tales, tossed in the waves,
Yet still they bask, in quirks they brave!

A hedgehog struts, with spines so tall,
Claiming the world, in his own hall.
His tiny crown, so proud he looks,
He's king of the forest, with little nooks!

Every stone, a character rich,
Holding secrets, comedy's itch.
With laughter echoing through the wood,
Nature's jests clearly understood!

As we wander, adventure awaits,
With whimsical stories that life creates.
In every rustle, a giggle peek,
Lost tales abound, mysterious yet cheek!

Hushed Murmurs Among the Branches

Whispers flutter in the breeze,
Squirrels gossip, sharing cheese.
Birds in feathers chirp their tunes,
While raccoons wear the latest boons.

Leaves flutter with a giggle bright,
As shadows play in fading light.
A fox wears socks, it's quite the sight,
In woodland fables, all feels right.

Beneath the boughs, a mouse does prance,
In dance of twirls, they take a chance.
The fireflies, like stars, take flight,
In this wild jest of sweet delight.

What chaos reigns in playful cheer,
As laughter echoes, drawing near.
In leafy nooks, the antics grow,
With each rustle, the fun will flow.

The Hidden Dance of Dusk

As twilight pulls her velvet cloak,
The badger juggles, what a joke!
The owls hoot, a rhythm grand,
While crickets tap a lively band.

The compass rose spins on a whim,
A rabbit leaps, the lights grow dim.
A hedgehog shows off pirouettes,
While moonlight brings its best duets.

Fireflies twinkle and take their bows,
In this quirky, merry house.
Each dancer wears a silly hat,
For nature knows the joy of that.

The curtain falls with laughter loud,
As dusk envelopes the woodland crowd.
In hidden glades, the secrets flow,
With every giggle, spirits glow.

Lurking Dreams of the Greenwood

A raccoon plots with mischief planned,
Dreams of pies so near at hand.
Each step is stealth, a cunning feat,
With giggles adrift on soft, green seat.

Squirrels dash to hide their loot,
In cozy nests, they take a snoot.
With acorns acting as their gold,
Fables unravel, just like told.

The nighttime brings a playful spark,
As creatures wander through the dark.
A frog attempts to sing a tune,
While mice compete for best costume.

With every nook, laughter resounds,
In leafy halls where joy abounds.
So in the dreams of woodland nights,
Life is a stage, and fun ignites.

Moonlit Reflections in Woodland Pools

The moon winks at a glassy lake,
Bubbles dance in a playful wake.
Frogs in tuxedos leap around,
In this reflection, joy is found.

The beavers grin, they craft and build,
While otters glide, their laughter spilled.
With splashes echoing off the trees,
All join in this grand soirée, with ease.

Starfish twirl in cosmic glee,
While turtles hum a melody.
With mirrored antics under night,
Each ripple brings more sheer delight.

In peaceful depths, the essence gleams,
Where moonlight births the wildest dreams.
With every splash, a story grows,
In woodland pools, where laughter flows.

The Language of Lost Light

In the park where the whispers play,
Squirrels debate the price of nuts all day.
They barter in giggles, a comical sight,
While rabbits roll over, claiming they're right.

The leaves shake with laughter, a rustle so loud,
As chipmunks perform for a gathering crowd.
With acorns as confetti, they throw up their hands,
And dance 'round the trunks, forming goofy bands.

The sun does its best to peek through the green,
But it's caught in a tussle, a match unforeseen.
It beams down its rays but the branches just sway,
And the giggles below send the light on its way.

A parade of odd critters, all lost in the fun,
Under branches where silly games brightly run.
The language of laughter, both bright and absurd,
Echoes through spaces where whimsy is stirred.

Secrets Woven in the Foliage

Among the green branches where secrets reside,
The birds hold council, their laughter can't hide.
They squawk and they chirp, with gossip so grand,
While a curious frog tries to understand.

The ants march in rhythm, a comical crew,
Discussing the merits of marching in two.
One slips on a leaf—oh, what a big blunder!
And the grass blades all laugh, as if torn asunder.

The sun drops a joke, but it's lost in the leaves,
As butterflies flutter and do as they please.
A squirrel strikes a pose, pretending to think,
While a deer peeks in, not wanting to blink.

With sunlight and laughter, the fabric is sewn,
In a tapestry woven of humor alone.
These secrets of mirth, by the daylight concealed,
Make the heart swell with joy, like a joke still unsealed.

Whispers in the Canopy

Up high in the branches where secrets may tease,
The wind tells a tale that brings giggles with ease.
The leaves sway and tumble, like sailors at play,
As the sun dims its lights in a silly ballet.

A raccoon dons glasses, pretending to read,
While owls hoot softly, their chatter they feed.
The chatterbox crickets join in with a song,
And the shadows grow lighter; it feels like a throng.

The fireflies flicker, a disco at dusk,
Each blink bursts with laughter; they're having a fuss.
Goofy old turtles offer sage advice,
That humor's the treasure that makes life so nice.

So gather 'neath branches where giggles ignite,
With whispers of joy that fill up the night.
The canopy's secrets are funny and bright,
As even the stars seem to twinkle with light.

Echoes of the Evening Light

As dusk draws its curtain, a comedy starts,
With critters on stage sharing flickering parts.
The hedgehogs in bow ties, they rattle their prongs,
While fireflies twirl, singing made-up songs.

A rabbit recites, with a dramatic flair,
While the audience giggles, forgetting their care.
The crickets keep beat, tapping feet with delight,
As the echo of laughter fills up the night.

Clouds lounge around, like they're part of the show,
As starlight joins in, putting on quite a glow.
It's a gathering place where the oddballs unite,
With jokes shared in whispers 'neath fading daylight.

So linger a moment, in this timeless scene,
Where the echoes of joy reign, buoyant and keen.
When the evening light dances, let your heart take flight,
In the charm of the critters and the echoes of night.

Organic Labyrinths of the Wise

In a park where squirrels conspire,
Wise owls sit, gossiping higher.
Rabbits hop in ridiculous circles,
Chasing tails, like eager turtles.

A hedgehog in glasses, reading a tome,
Points out routes, leading them home.
Yet they wander off to play ball,
While the wise owl rolls his eyes at them all.

The trees giggle in the soft breeze,
As the raccoons throw crumbs to tease.
Chasing acorns, they split their pants,
Who knew oak trees could cause such chance?

And when the sun sets, they all must flee,
To avoid tales spun by the beetle's decree.
For laughter's the key in this wild spree,
In the playground where nature's set free.

Entranced by the Lush Surrounds

In leafy lanes where dreams do hide,
Pigeons prance, sharing their pride.
Chasing shadows cast by the sun,
The antics here are never done.

Lizards lounging, sunbathing galore,
Shaking tails and begging for more.
They boast about their sun-kissed days,
While crickets serenade in playful ways.

The flowers nod in a witty debate,
"Who's more fragrant, you or your mate?"
Bees buzz in, adding to the fun,
"You both smell sweet, now let's run!"

As night falls, the stars twinkle bright,
Fireflies flash, a luminous sight.
With laughter echoing, a silly sound,
In this whimsical world, joy abounds!

Balance of Silence and Sound

In the depths of the forest, a joke takes flight,
As mushrooms giggle at passing light.
The trees whisper secrets, oh so sly,
While butterflies flutter, with a wink of an eye.

An echoing laugh from a nearby stream,
Fish are plotting their watery scheme.
"Who can jump higher on this fine day?"
It's a rib-tickling contest on display.

The wind rustles leaves, in a playful chase,
While beetles break dance at their own pace.
Frantic squirrels gather, devising a prank,
And laughter erupts from each leafy flank.

So come hear the beat of nature's song,
Where silliness flows and you can't go wrong.
In this world of jest, no frown can be found,
Just a merry medley of silence and sound.

Narratives of the Whispering Woods

The stories unfold where the breezes sway,
As leaves conspire in their clever play.
A fox in a hat tells tales of surprise,
While owls exchange winks with wise little eyes.

A rabbit with socks struts down the aisle,
Claiming that style is his secret file.
The other critters giggle and tease,
As they stop to admire the fashion with ease.

At twilight, the crickets form a band,
With grasshoppers joining at their command.
Harmonies created in joyous delight,
As the forest holds its breath for the night.

With laughter and stories, the stars come out,
Winking and glimmering, without any doubt.
In this whispering world, where fun is the game,
Adventure awaits, with laughter to claim.

Veils of Twilight's Embrace

In the dusk when the critters play,
A squirrel in a tutu steals the day.
With a leap and a twirl, he makes his dash,
Is that a ballet or just a crash?

The frogs hold a concert, they break into song,
But their tunes are quite silly, they don't last long.
A toad plays the drums, with a stick from a tree,
While the crickets cheer on, sipping sweet tea.

A hedgehog attempts a pirouette high,
But ends up in a bush, oh my, oh my!
With laughter echoing, the night greets the crew,
Who knew twilight's veil could host such a zoo?

Every night brings a waltz, a jig, and a slide,
Amidst leaves and laughter, we dance side by side.
In this playful embrace of the fading light,
We find joy in mischief, the heart takes its flight.

Dappled Silence on the Forest Floor

Through leaves, little feet scurry and race,
As a chipmunk discovers a hidden space.
With acorns as treasures, he digs with flair,
But ends up quite stuck in a patch of despair.

A rabbit in sneakers hops with such grace,
Chasing shadows that vanish, at quite a pace.
He trips on a root, does a somersault twist,
And lands in a puddle with a great splash and mist!

A turtle named Gary, older and wise,
Claims the best sunbeam, oh what a prize!
But a squirrel steals it, they argue and fight,
Who knew that warm rays could spark such a night?

The floor is alive with giggles and cheer,
As nature unveils its comical sphere.
With dappled light playing on all who explore,
The silent whispers turn to laughter galore.

Secrets of the Leafy Giants

Beneath leafy arms, a secret is shared,
Where the wise old owl seems rather unprepared.
He fumbles his words, trying to sound grand,
But ends up confusing each critter and band.

A raccoon with jokes tries to lighten the mood,
But his humor is stale, instead of real food.
He serves up some berries, a curious feast,
But they're past their prime, oh what a beast!

The trees softly giggle, their laughter, a breeze,
As the forest holds tales of blunders with ease.
With every mishap, the night comes alive,
In the company of friends, hilarity thrives.

Under the branches, where secrets are spun,
A dance of mishaps, oh what fun!
These giants may sway, but they never do frown,
As they shelter the laughter that's shared all around.

Flickering Phantoms in the Grove

In the grove, tiny sprites dance on the breeze,
With twinkles that shimmer, their grooves aim to please.
Yet they trip on each other, all tangled in flight,
A waltz turning wild, oh what a sight!

The fireflies chatter, their gossip a buzz,
Spilling secrets of squirrels and what they because.
A dance-off erupts, who's the brightest of all?
But they all end up tangled, they stumble and fall.

A shadowy figure, just a trickster's guise,
A raccoon in costume, wearing sunglasses so wise.
He prances and struts, with a caper so bold,
Making all of the creatures giggle, uncontrolled!

With whimsy afoot, the night spins away,
As phantoms of laughter come out to play.
In the whims of the grove, with ridiculous glee,
We join in the folly, forever carefree.

www.ingramcontent.com/pod-product-compliance
Lightning Source LLC
Chambersburg PA
CBHW071824160426
43209CB00003B/203